Foundation
Stones *to*
Happiness
and Success

JAMES ALLEN TITLES

Foundation Stones *to* Happiness *and* Success

James Allen

Published 2019 by Gildan Media LLC
aka G&D Media
www.GandDmedia.com

Design by Meghan Day Healey of Story Horse, LLC

Library of Congress Cataloging-in-Publication Data is available upon request

ISBN: 978-1-7225-0252-2

10   9   8   7   6   5   4   3   2   1

More Good is the recompense of Good;
More Virtue is the reward of Virtue;
More capacity is the crown of Use.
In Goodness, Virtue, and the wise use of all our
    powers is all happiness.
Other forms of happiness are fleeting,
But this abides, and does not pass away.

Contents

Foreword

How does a man begin the building of a house? He first secures a plan of the proposed edifice, and then proceeds to build according to the plan, scrupulously following it in every detail, beginning with the foundation. Should he neglect the beginning—the beginning on a mathematical plan—his labor would be wasted, and his building, should it reach completion without tumbling to pieces, would be insecure and worthless. The same law holds good in any important work: the right beginning and first essential is *a definite mental plan on which to build*.

Nature will have no slipshod work, no slovenliness, and she annihilates confusion, or rather, confusion is in itself annihilated. Order, definiteness, purpose, eternally prevail, and he who in his operations ignores these mathematical elements at once deprives himself of substantiality, completeness, happiness, and success.

—James Allen

Editor's Preface

This is one of the last manuscripts written by James Allen. Like all his works it is eminently practical. He never wrote *theories*, or for the sake of writing; but he wrote when he had a message, and it became a message *only when he had lived it out in his own life*, and knew that it was good. Thus he wrote *facts*, which he had proven by practice.

To live out the teaching of this book faithfully in every detail of life will lead one to more than happiness and success—even to Blessedness, Satisfaction, and Peace.

—Lily L. Allen
Bryngoleu,
Ilfracombe, England

Right Principles

It is wise to know what comes first, and what to do first. To begin anything in the middle or at the end is to make a muddle of it. The athlete who began by breaking the tape would not receive the prize. He must begin by facing the starter and toeing the mark, and even then a good start is important if he is to win. The pupil does not begin with algebra and literature, but with counting and A B C. So in life—the business men who begin at the bottom, achieve the more enduring success; and the religious men who reach the highest heights of spiritual knowledge and wisdom are they who have stooped to serve a patient apprenticeship to the humbler tasks, and have not scorned the common experiences of humanity, or overlooked the lessons to be learned from them.

The first things in a sound life—and therefore in a truly happy and successful life—are *right principles*. Without right principles to begin with, there will be wrong practices to follow with, and a bungled and wretched life to end with. All the Infinite variety of calculations which tabulate the commerce and science of the world, come out of the ten figures; all the hundreds of thousands of books which constitute the literature of the world, and perpetuate its thought and genius, are built up from the twenty-six letters. The greatest astronomer cannot ignore the ten simple figures. The profoundest man of genius cannot dispense with the twenty-six simple characters. The fundamentals in all things are few and simple; yet without them there is no knowledge and no achievement. The fundamentals—the basic principles—in life, or true living, are also few and simple, and to learn them thoroughly, and study how to apply them to all the details of life, is to avoid confusion, and to secure a substantial foundation for the orderly building up of an invincible character and a permanent success; and to succeed in comprehending those principles in their innumerable ramifications in the labyrinth of conduct, is to become a Master of Life.

The first principles in life are principles of conduct. To name them is easy. As mere words they are on all men's lips, but as fixed sources of action, admitting of no compromise, few have learned them. In this short talk I will deal with five only of these principles. These five are among the simplest of the root principles of life, but they are those that come nearest to the every-day life, for they touch the artisan, the business man, the householder, the citizen, at every point. Not one of them can be dispensed with but at severe cost, and he who perfects himself in their application will rise superior to many of the troubles and failures of life, and will come into these springs and currents of thought which flow harmoniously toward the regions of enduring success. First among these principles is:

Duty

A much-hackneyed word, I know, but it contains a rare jewel for him who will seek it by assiduous application. The principle of duty means strict adherence to one's own business, and just as strict non-interference in the business of others. The man who is continually instructing others, gratis, how to manage their affairs, is the one who most mismanages his own.

Duty also means undivided attention to the matter in hand, intelligent concentration of the mind on the work to be done; it includes all that is meant by thoroughness, exactness, and efficiency.

The details of duties differ with individuals, and each man should know his own duty better than he knows his neighbor's, and better than his neighbor knows his; but although the working details differ, the principle is always the same. Who has mastered the demands of duty?

Honesty

Honesty is the next principle. It means not cheating or overcharging another. It involves the absence of all trickery, lying and deception by word, look or gesture. It includes sincerity, the saying what you mean, and the meaning what you say. It scorns cringing policy and shining compliment. It builds up good reputations, and good reputations build up good businesses, and bright joy accompanies well-earned success. Who has scaled the heights of Honesty?

Economy

Economy is the third principle. The conservation of one's financial resources is merely the vestibule leading toward the more spacious chambers of true economy. It means, as well, the husbanding of one's physical vitality and mental resources. It demands the conservation of energy by the avoidance of enervating self-indulgences and sensual habits. It holds for its follower, strength, endurance, vigilance, and capacity to achieve. It bestows great power on him who learns it well. Who has realized in all its force the supreme strength of Economy?

Liberality

Liberality follows economy. It is not opposed to it. Only the man of economy can afford to be generous. The spendthrift, whether in money, vitality, or mental energy, wastes so much on his own miserable pleasures as to have none left to bestow upon others. The giving of money is the smallest part of liberality. There is a giving of thoughts, and deeds, and sympathy, the bestowing of good-will, the being generous toward calumniators and opponents. It is a principle that begets a noble, far-reaching influence. It brings loving friends and stanch comrades, and is the foe of loneliness and despair. Who has measured the breadth of Liberality?

Self-control

Self-control is the last of these five principles, yet the most important. Its neglect is the cause of vast misery, innumerable failures, and tens of thousands of financial, physical, and mental wrecks.

◇ ◇ ◇

Show me the business man who loses his temper with a customer over some trivial matter, and I will show you a man who, by that condition of mind, is doomed to failure. If all men practised even the initial stages of self-control, anger, with its consuming and destroying fire, would be unknown. The lessons of patience, purity, gentleness, kindness and steadfastness which are contained in the principle of self-control, are slowly learned by men, yet until they are truly learned, a man's character and success are uncertain and insecure. Where is the man who has perfected himself in self-control? Wherever he may be, he is a Master indeed.

The five principles are five practices, five avenues to achievement, and five sources of knowledge. It is an old saying and a good rule that "Practice makes perfect," and he who would make his own the wisdom which is inherent in those principles, must not merely have them on his lips, they must be established in his heart. To know them, and receive what they alone can bring, he must *do* them, and give them out in his actions.

Sound Methods

From the five foregoing Right Principles, when they are truly apprehended and practised, will issue *Sound Methods*. Right principles are manifested in harmonious action, and method is to life what law is to the universe. Everywhere in the universe there is the harmonious adjustment of parts, and it is this symmetry and harmony that reveals a cosmos, as distinguished from chaos. So in human life, the difference between a true life and a false, between one purposeful and effective and one purposeless and weak, is one of method. The false life is an incoherent jumble of thoughts, passions, and actions; the true life is an orderly adjustment of all its parts. It is all the difference between a mass of lumber and a smoothly working efficient machine. A piece of machinery in perfect working order is not only a useful, but an admirable and attractive thing; but when its parts are all out of gear, and refuse to be readjusted, its usefulness and attractiveness are gone, and it is thrown on the scrap-heap. Likewise a life perfectly adjusted in all its parts so as to achieve the highest point of efficiency, is not only a powerful, but an excellent and beautiful thing; whereas a life confused, inconsistent, discordant, is a deplorable exhibition of wasted energy.

If life is to be truly lived, method must enter into, and regulate, every detail of it, as it enters and regulates every detail of the wondrous universe of which we form a part. One of the distinguishing differences between a wise man and a foolish is, that the wise man pays careful attention to the smallest things, while the foolish man slurs over them, or neglects them altogether. Wisdom consists in maintaining things in their right relations, in keeping all things, the smallest as well as the greatest, in their proper places and times. To violate order is to produce confusion and discord, and *unhappiness* is but another name for discord.

The good business man knows that system is three parts of success, and that disorder means failure. The wise man knows that disciplined, methodical living is three parts of happiness, and that looseness means misery. What is a fool but one who thinks carelessly, acts rashly and lives loosely? What is a wise man but one who thinks carefully, acts calmly, and lives consistently!

The true method does not end with the orderly arrangement of the material things and external relations of life; this is but its beginning; it enters into the adjustment of the mind—the discipline of the passions, the elimination and choice of words in speech, the logical arrangement of the thoughts, and the selection of right actions.

To achieve a life rendered sound, successful, and sweet by the pursuance of sound methods, one must begin, not by neglect of the little every-day things, but by assiduous attention to them. Thus the hour of rising is important, and its regularity significant; as also are the time of retiring to rest, and the number of hours given to sleep. Between the regularity and irregularity of meals, and the care and carelessness with which they are eaten, is all the difference between a good and bad digestion (with all that this implies) and an irritable or comfortable frame of mind, with its train of good or bad consequences, for, attaching to these meal-times and meal-ways are matters of both physiological and psychological significance. The due division of hours for business and for play, not confusing the two, the orderly fitting in of all the details of one's business, times for solitude, for silent thought and for effective action, for eating and for abstinence—all these things must have their lawful place in the life of him whose "daily round" is to proceed with the minimum degree of friction, who is to get the most of usefulness, influence, and joy out of life.

But all this is but the beginning of that comprehensive method which embraces the whole life and being. When this smooth order and logical consistency is extended to the words and actions, to the thoughts and desires, then wisdom emerges from folly, and out of weakness comes power sublime. When a man so orders his mind as to produce a beautiful working harmony between all its parts, then he reaches the highest wisdom, the highest efficiency, the highest happiness.

But this is the end; and he who would reach the end must begin at the beginning. He must systematize and render logical and smooth the smallest details of his life, proceeding step by step toward the finished accomplishment. But each step will yield its own particular measure of strength and gladness.

To sum up, method produces that smoothness which goes with strength and efficiency. Discipline is method applied to the mind. It produces that calmness which goes with power and happiness. Method is *working* by rule; discipline is *living* by rule. But working and living are not separate; they are but two aspects of character, of life.

Therefore, be orderly in work; be accurate in speech; be logical in thought. Between these and slovenliness, inaccuracy, and confusion, is the difference between success and failure, music and discord, happiness and misery.

The adoption of sound methods of working, acting, thinking,—in a word, of *living*, is the surest and safest foundation for sound health, sound success, sound peace of mind. The foundation of unsound methods will be found to be unstable, and to yield fear and unrest even while it appears to succeed; when failure comes, it is grievous indeed.

True Actions

Following on Right Principles and Methods, come True Actions. One who is striving to grasp true principles and work with sound methods will soon come to perceive that details of conduct cannot be overlooked,—that, indeed, those details are fundamentally distinctive or creative, according to their nature, and are, therefore, of deep significance and comprehensive importance; and this perception and knowledge of the nature and power of passing actions will gradually open and grow within him as an added vision, a new revelation. As he acquires this insight, his progress will be more rapid, his pathway in life more sure, his days more serene and peaceful; in all things he will go the true and direct way, unswayed and untroubled by the external forces that play around and about him. Not that he will be indifferent to the welfare and happiness of those about him; that is quite another thing; but he will be indifferent to their opinions, to their ignorance, to their ungoverned passions. By *True Actions*, indeed, is meant acting rightly toward others, and the right-doer knows that actions in accordance with truth are but for the happiness of those about him, and he will do them even though an occasion may arise when some one near to him may advise or implore him to do otherwise.

True actions may easily be distinguished from false by all who wish so to distinguish in order that they may avoid false action, and adopt true. As in the material world we distinguish things by their form, color, size, etc., choosing those things which we require, and putting by those things which are not useful to us, so in the spiritual world of deeds, we can distinguish between those that are bad and those that are good by their nature, their aim, and their effect, and can choose and adopt those that are good, and ignore those that are bad.

In all forms of progress, *avoidance of the bad* always precedes *acceptance and knowledge of the good*, just as a child at school learns to do its lessons right by having repeatedly pointed out to it how it has done them wrong. If one does not know what is wrong and how to avoid it, how can he know what is right and how to practice it? Bad, or untrue, actions are those that spring from a consideration of one's own happiness only, and ignore the happiness of others, that arise in violent disturbances of the mind and unlawful desires, or that call for concealment in order to avoid undesirable complications. Good, or true, actions are those that spring from a consideration for others, that arise in calm reason and harmonious thought framed on moral principles, or that will not involve the doer in shameful consequences if brought into the full light of day.

The right-doer will avoid those acts of personal pleasure and gratification which by their nature bring annoyance, pain, or suffering to others, no matter how insignificant those actions may appear to be. He will begin by putting away these; he will gain a knowledge of the unselfish and true by first sacrificing the selfish and untrue. He will learn not to speak or act in anger, or envy, or resentment, but will study how to control his mind, and will restore it to calmness before acting; and, most important of all, he will avoid, as he would the drinking of deadly poison, those acts of trickery, deceit, double-dealing in order to gain some personal profit or advantage, and which lead, sooner or later, to exposure and shame for the doer of them. If a man is prompted to do a thing which he needs to conceal, and which he would not lawfully and frankly defend if it were examined of witness, he should know by that, that it is a wrong act, and therefore to be abandoned without one further moment of consideration.

The carrying out of this principle of honesty and sincerity of action, too, will further lead him into such a path of thoughtfulness in right-doing as will enable him to avoid doing those things which would involve him in the deceptive practices of other people. Before signing papers, or entering into verbal or written arrangements, or engaging himself to others in any way at their request, particularly if they be strangers, he will first inquire into the nature of the work or undertaking, and so, enlightened, he will know exactly what to do, and will be fully aware of the import of his action. To the right-doer, *thoughtlessness* is a crime. Thousands of actions done with good intent lead to disastrous consequences because they are acts of thoughtlessness, and it is well said that "the way to hell is paved with good intentions." The man of true actions is, above all things, thoughtful; "Be ye therefore wise as serpents and harmless as doves."

The term *Thoughtlessness* covers a wide field in the realm of deeds. It is only by increasing in thoughtfulness that a man can come to understand the nature of actions, and, can, thereby, acquire the power of *always doing that which is right*. It is impossible for a man to be thoughtful and act foolishly. Thoughtfulness embraces wisdom.

It is not enough that an action is prompted by a good impulse or intention; it must arise in *thoughtful consideration* if it is to be a true action; and the man who wishes to be permanently happy in himself and a power for good to others must concern himself only with true actions. "I did it with the best of intentions" is a poor excuse from one who has thoughtlessly involved himself in the wrongdoing of others. His bitter experience should teach him to act more thoughtfully in the future.

True actions can only spring from a true mind; and therefore while a man is learning to distinguish and choose between the false and the true, he is correcting and perfecting his mind, and is thereby rendering it more harmonious and felicitous, more efficient and powerful. As he acquires the "inner eye" to clearly distinguish the right in all the details of life, and the faith and knowledge to do it, he will realize that he is building the house of his character and life upon a rock which the winds of failure and the storms of persecution can never undermine.

True Speech

Truth is known by practice only. Without sincerity there can be no knowledge of Truth; and true speech is the beginning of all sincerity. Truth in all its native beauty and original simplicity consists in abandoning and not doing all those things which are untrue, and in embracing and doing all those things which are true. True speech is therefore one of the elementary beginnings in the life of Truth. Falsehood, and all forms of deception; slander and all forms of evil-speaking—these must be totally abandoned and abolished before the mind can receive even a small degree of spiritual enlightenment. The liar and slanderer is lost in darkness; so deep is his darkness that he cannot distinguish between good and evil, and he persuades himself that his lying and evil-speaking are necessary and good, that he is thereby protecting himself and other people.

Let the would-be student of "higher things" look to himself and beware of self-delusion. If he is given to uttering words that deceive, or to speaking evil of others—if he speaks in insincerity, envy, or malice—then he has not yet begun to study higher things. He may be studying metaphysics, or miracles, or psychic phenomena, or astral wonders—he may be studying how to commune with invisible beings, to travel invisibly during sleep, or to produce curious phenomena—he may even study spirituality theoretically and as a mere book study, but if he is a deceiver and a back-biter, the higher life is hidden from him. For the higher things are these—*uprightness, sincerity, innocence, purity, kindness, gentleness, faithfulness, humility, patience, pity, sympathy, self-sacrifice, joy, goodwill, love*—and he who would study them, know them, and make them his own, must practice them, there is no other way.

Lying and evil-speaking belong to the lowest forms of spiritual ignorance, and there can be no such thing as spiritual enlightenment while they are practised. Their parents are selfishness and hatred.

Slander is akin to lying, but it is even more subtle, as it is frequently associated with indignation, and by assuming more successfully the appearance of truth, it ensnares many who would not tell a deliberate falsehood. For there are two sides to slander—there is *the making or repeating of it*, and there is *the listening to it and acting upon it*. The slanderer would be powerless without a listener.

Evil words require an ear that is receptive to evil in which they may fall, before they can flourish; therefore he who listens to a slander, who believes it, and allows himself to be influenced against the person whose character and reputation are defamed, is in the same position as the one who framed or repeated the evil report. The evil-speaker is a positive slanderer; the evil-listener is a passive slanderer. The two are co-operators in the propagation of evil.

Slander is a common vice and a dark and deadly one. An evil report begins in ignorance, and pursues its blind way in darkness. It generally takes its rise in a misunderstanding. Some one feels that he, or she, has been badly treated, and, filled with indignation and resentment, unburdens himself to his friends and others in vehement language, exaggerating the enormity of the supposed offence on account of the feeling of injury by which he is possessed; his listeners, without hearing *the other person's* version of what has taken place, and on no other proof than the violent words of an angry man or woman, become cold in their attitude toward the one spoken against, and repeat to others what they have been told, and as such repetition is always more or less inaccurate, a distorted and altogether untrue report is soon passing from mouth to mouth.

It is because slander is such a common vice that it can work the suffering and injury that it does. It is because so many (not deliberate wrong-doers, and unconscious of the nature of the evil into which they so easily fall) are ready to allow themselves to be influenced against one whom they have hitherto regarded as honorable, that an evil report can do its deadly work. Yet its work is only amongst those who have not altogether acquired the virtue of true speech, the cause of which is a truth-loving mind. When one who has not entirely freed himself from repeating or believing an evil report about another, hears of an evil report about himself, his mind becomes aflame with burning resentment, his sleep is broken and his peace of mind is destroyed. He thinks the cause of all his suffering is in the other man and what that man has said about him, and is ignorant of the truth that *the root and cause of his suffering lies in his own readiness to believe an evil report about another.* The virtuous man—he who has attained to true speech, and whose mind is sealed against even the appearance of evil-speaking—cannot be injured and disturbed about any evil reports concerning himself; and although his reputation may for a time be stained *in the minds of those who are prone to suggestions of evil,* his integrity remains untouched and his character unsoiled; for no one can be stained by the evil deeds of another, but only by his own wrong-doing. And so, through all misrepresentation, misunderstanding, and contumely, he is untroubled and unrevengeful; his sleep is undisturbed, and his mind remains in peace.

True speech is the beginning of a pure, wise and well-ordered life. If one would attain to purity of life, if he would lessen the evil and suffering of the world, let him abandon falsehood and slander in thought and word, let him avoid even the appearance of these things, for there are no lies and slanders so deadly as those which are half-truths, and let him not be a participant in evil-speaking by listening to it. Let him also have compassion on the evil-speaker, knowing how such a one is binding himself to suffering and unrest; for no liar can know the bliss of Truth; no slanderer can enter the kingdom of peace.

By the words which he utters is a man's spiritual condition declared; by these also is he finally and infallibly adjudged, for as the Divine Master of the Christian world has declared: "By thy words shalt thou be justified, and by thy words shalt thou be condemned."

Equal-Mindedness

To be equally minded is to be peacefully minded, for a man cannot be said to have arrived at peace who allows his mind to be disturbed and thrown off the balance by occurrences.

The man of wisdom is dispassionate, and meets all things with the calmness of a mind in repose and free from prejudice. He is not a partisan, having put away passion, and he is always at peace with himself and the world, not taking sides nor defending himself, but sympathizing with all.

The partisan is so convinced that his own opinion and his own side are right, and all that goes contrary to them is wrong, that he cannot think there is any good in the other opinion and the other side. He lives in a continual fever of attack and defence, and has no knowledge of the quiet peace of an equal mind.

The equal-minded man watches himself in order to check and overcome even the appearance of passion and prejudice in his mind, and by so doing he develops sympathy for others, and comes to understand their position and particular state of mind; and as he comes to understand others, he perceives the folly of condemning them and opposing himself to them. Thus there grows up in his heart a divine charity which cannot be limited, but which is extended to all things that live and strive and suffer.

When a man is under the sway of passion and prejudice he is spiritually blind. Seeing nothing but good in his own side, and nothing but evil in the other, he cannot see anything as it really is, not even his own side; and not understanding himself, he cannot understand the hearts of others, and thinks it is right that he should condemn them. Thus there grows up in his heart a dark hatred for those who refuse to see with him and who condemn him in return, he becomes separated from his fellow-men, and Confines himself to a narrow torture-chamber of his own making.

Sweet and peaceful are the days of the equal-minded man, fruitful in good, and rich in manifold blessings. Guided by wisdom, he avoids those pathways which lead down to hatred and sorrow and pain, and takes those which lead up to love and peace and bliss. The occurrences of life do not trouble him, nor does he grieve over those things which are regarded by mankind as grievous, but which must befall all men in the ordinary course of nature. He is neither elated by success nor cast down by failure. He sees the events of his life arrayed in their proper proportions, and can find no room for selfish wishes or vain regrets, for vain anticipations and childish disappointments.

And how is this equal-mindedness—this blessed state of mind and life—acquired? Only by overcoming one's self, only by purifying one's own heart, for the purification of the heart leads to unbiassed comprehension, unbiassed comprehension leads to equal-mindedness, and equal-mindedness leads to peace. The impure man is swept helplessly away on the waves of passion; the pure man guides himself into the harbor of rest. The fool says, "I have an opinion"; the wise man goes about his business.

Good Results

A considerable portion of the happenings of life come to us without any *direct* choosing on our part, and such happenings are generally regarded as having no relation to our will or character, but as appearing fortuitously, as occurring without a cause. Thus one is spoken of as being "lucky," and another "unlucky," the inference being that each has received something which he never earned, never caused. Deeper thought and a clearer insight into life convince us, however, that nothing happens without a cause, and that cause and effect are always related in perfect adjustment and harmony. This being so, every happening directly affecting us is intimately related to our own will and character, is, indeed, an effect justly related to a cause having its seat in our consciousness. In a word, involuntary happenings of life are the results of our own thoughts and deeds. This, I admit, is not apparent on the surface, but what fundamental law, even in the physical universe, is so apparent? If thought, investigation, and experiment are necessary to the discovery of the principles which relate one material atom to another, even so are they imperative to the perception and understanding of the mode of action which relate one mental condition to another; and such modes, such laws, are known by the right-doer, by him who has acquired an understanding mind by the practice of true actions.

We reap as we sow. Those things which come to us, though not by our own *choosing*, are by our *causing*. The drunkard did not choose the delirium tremens or insanity which overtook him, but he caused it by his own deeds. In this case the law is plain to all minds, but where it is not so plain, it is none the less true. Within ourselves is the deep-seated cause of all our sufferings, the spring of all our joys. Alter the inner world of thoughts, and the outer world of events will cease to bring you sorrow; make the heart pure, and to you all things will be pure, all occurrences happy and in true order.

Within yourselves deliverance must be sought,
*   Each man his prison makes.*
Each hath such lordship as the loftiest ones;
*   Nay, for with Powers above, around, below*
As with all flesh and whatsoever lives,
*   Act maketh joy or woe.*

Our life is good or bad, enslaved or free, according to its causation in our thoughts, for out of these thoughts spring all our deeds; and from these deeds come equitable results. We cannot seize good results violently, like a thief, and claim and enjoy them, but we can bring them to pass by setting in motion the causes within ourselves.

Men strive for money, sigh for happiness, and would gladly possess wisdom, yet fail to secure these things, while they see others to whom these blessings appear to come unbidden. The reason is that they have generated causes which prevent the fulfilment of their wishes and efforts.

Each life is a perfectly woven net-work of causes and effects, of efforts (or lack of efforts) and results, and good results can only be reached by initiating good efforts, good causes. The doer of true actions, who pursues sound methods grounded on right principles, will not need to strive and struggle for good results; they will be there as the effects of his righteous rule of life. He will reap the fruit of his own actions and the reaping will be in gladness and peace.

This truth of sowing and reaping in the moral sphere is a simple one, yet men are slow to understand and accept it. We have been told by a Wise One that "the children of darkness are wiser in their day than the children of light," and who would expect, in the material world, to reap and eat where he had not sown and planted? Or who would expect to reap wheat in the field where he had sown tares, and would fall to weeping and complaining if he did not? Yet this is just what men do in the spiritual field of mind and deed. They do evil, and expect to get from it good, and when the bitter harvesting comes in all its ripened fulness, they fall into despair, and bemoan the hardness and injustice of their lot, usually attributing it to the evil deeds of others, refusing even to admit the possibility of its cause being hidden in themselves, in their own thoughts and deeds. The children of light—those who are searching for the fundamental principles of right living with a view to making themselves into wise and happy beings—must train themselves to observe this law of cause and effect in thought, word and deed, as implicitly and obediently as the gardener obeys the law of sowing and reaping. He does not even question the law; he recognizes and obeys it. When the wisdom which he instinctively practises in his garden, is practised by men in the garden of their minds—when the law of the sowing of deeds is so fully recognized that it can no longer be doubted or questioned—then it will be just as faithfully followed by the sowing of those actions which will bring about a reaping of happiness and well-being for all. As the children of matter obey the laws of matter, so let the children of spirit obey the laws of spirit, for the law of matter and the law of spirit are one; they are but two aspects of one thing; the outworking of one principle in opposite directions.

If we observe right principles or causes, wrong effects cannot possibly accrue. If we pursue sound methods, no shoddy thread can find its way into the web of our life, no rotten brick enter into the building of our character to render it insecure; and if we do true actions, what but good results can come to pass; for to say that good causes can produce bad effects is to say that nettles can be reaped from a sowing of corn.

He who orders his life along the moral lines thus briefly enunciated, will attain to such a state of insight and equilibrium as to render him permanently happy and perennially glad; all his efforts will be seasonably planted; all the issues of his life will be good, and though he may not become a millionaire—as indeed he will have no desire to become such—he will acquire the gift of peace, and true success will wait upon him as its commanding master.

James Allen:
A Memoir

By Lily L. Allen

from *The Epoch* (February–March 1912)

Unto pure devotion
Devote thyself: with perfect meditation
Comes perfect act, and the right-hearted rise—
More certainly because they seek no gain—
Forth from the bands of body, step by step.
To highest seats of bliss.

James Allen was born in Leicester, England, on November 28th, 1864. His father, at one time a very prosperous manufacturer, was especially fond of "Jim," and before great financial failures overtook him, he would often look at the delicate, refined boy, poring over his books, and would say, "My boy, I'll make a scholar of you."

The Father was a high type of man intellectually, and a great reader, so could appreciate the evident thirst for education and knowledge which he observed in his quiet studious boy.

As a young child he was very delicate and nervous, often suffering untold agony during his school days through the misunderstanding harshness of some of his school teachers, and others with whom he was forced to associate, though he retained always the tenderest memories of others—one or two of his teachers in particular, who no doubt are still living.

He loved to get alone with his books, and many a time he has drawn a vivid picture for me, of the hours he spent with his precious books in his favourite corner by the home fire; his father, whom he dearly loved, in his arm chair opposite also deeply engrossed in his favourite authors. On such evenings he would question his father on some of the profound thoughts that surged through his soul— thoughts he could scarcely form into words—and the father, unable to answer, would gaze at him long over his spectacles, and at last say: "My boy, my boy, you have lived before"—and when the boy eagerly but reverently would suggest an answer to his own question, the father would grow silent and thoughtful, as though he *sensed* the future man and his mission, as he looked at the boy and listened to his words—and many a time he was heard to remark, "Such knowledge comes not in one short life."

There were times when the boy startled those about him into a deep concern for his health, and they would beg him not to *think so much*, and in after years he often smiled when he recalled how his father would say—"Jim, we will have you in the Churchyard soon, if you think so much."

Not that he was by any means unlike other boys where games were concerned. He could play leapfrog and marbles with the best of them, and those who knew him as a man—those who were privileged to meet him at "Bryngoleu"—will remember how he could enter into a game with all his heart. Badminton he delighted in during the summer evenings, or whenever he felt he could.

About three years after our marriage, when our little Nora was about eighteen months old, and he about thirty-three, I realized a great change coming over him, and knew that he was renouncing everything that most men hold dear that he might find Truth, and lead the weary sin-stricken world to Peace. He at that time commenced the practice of rising early in the morning, at times long before daylight, that he might go out on the hills—like One of old—to commune with God, and meditate on Divine things. I do not claim to have understood him fully in those days. The light in which he lived and moved was far too white for my earth-bound eyes to see, and a *sense of it only* was beginning to dawn upon me. But I knew I dare not stay him or hold him back, though at times my woman's heart cried out to do so, waiting him all my own, and not then understanding his divine mission.

Then came his first book, "From Poverty to Power." This book is considered by many his best book. It has passed into many editions, and tens of thousands have been sold all over the world, both authorized and pirated editions, for perhaps no author's works have been more pirated than those of James Allen.

As a private secretary he worked from 9 a.m. to 6 p.m., and used every moment out of office writing his books. Soon after the publication of "From Poverty to Power" came "All These Things Added," and then "As a Man Thinketh," a book perhaps better known and more widely read than any other from his pen.

About this time, too, the "Light of Reason" was founded and he gave up all his time to the work of editing the Magazine, at the same time carrying on a voluminous correspondence with searchers after Truth all over the world. And ever as the years went by he kept straight on, and never once looked back or swerved from the path of holiness. Oh, it was a blessed thing indeed to be the chosen one to walk by the side of his earthly body, and to watch the glory dawning upon him!

He took a keen interest in many scientific subjects, and always eagerly read the latest discovery in astronomy, and he delighted in geology and botany. Among his favourite books I find Shakespeare, Milton, Emerson, Browning, The Bhagavad-Gita, the Tao-Tea-King of Lao-Tze, the Light of Asia, the Gospel of Buddha, Walt Whitman, Dr. Bucke's Cosmic Consciousness, and the Holy Bible.

He might have written on a wide range of subjects had he chosen to do so, and was often asked for articles on many questions outside his particular work, but he refused to comply, consecrating his whole thought and effort to preach the Gospel of Peace.

When physical suffering overtook him he never once complained, but grandly and patiently bore his pain, hiding it from those around him, and only we who knew and loved him so well, and his kind, tender Doctor, knew how greatly he suffered. And yet he stayed not; still he rose before the dawn to meditate, and commune with God; still he sat at his desk and wrote those words of Light and Life which will ring down through the ages, calling men and women from their sins and sorrows to peace and rest.

Always strong in his complete manhood, though small of stature physically, and as gentle as he was strong, no one ever heard an angry word from those kind lips. Those who served him adored him; those who had business dealings with him trusted and honoured him. Ah! how much my heart prompts me to write of his self-sacrificing life, his tender words, his gentle deeds, his knowledge and his wisdom. But why? Surely there is no need, for do not his books speak in words written by his own hand, and will they not speak to generations yet to come?

About Christmas time I saw the change coming, and understood it not—blind! blind! blind! I could not think it possible that *he* should be taken and *I* left.

But we three—as if we knew—clung closer to each other, and loved one another with a greater love—if that were possible—than ever before. Look at his portrait given with the January "Epoch," and reproduced again in this, and you will see that even then our Beloved, our Teacher and Guide, was letting go his hold on the physical. He was leaving us then, and we didn't know it. Often I had urged him to stop work awhile and rest, but he always gave me the same answer, "My darling, when I stop I must go, don't try to stay my hand."

And so he worked on, until that day, Friday, January 12, 1912, when, about one o'clock he sat down in his chair, and looking at me with a great compassion and yearning in those blessed eyes, he cried out, as he stretched out his arms to me, *"Oh, I have finished, I have finished, I can go no further, I have done."*

Need I say that everything that human aid and human skill could do was done to keep him still with us. Of those last few days I dare scarcely write. How could my pen describe them? And when we knew the end was near, with his dear hands upon my head in blessing, he gave his work and his beloved people into my hands, charging me to bless and help them, until I received the call to give up my stewardship!

"I will help you," he said, "and if I can I shall come to you and be with you often."

Words, blessed words of love and comfort, *for my heart alone* often came from his lips, and a sweet smile ever came over the pale calm face when our little Nora came to kiss him and speak loving words to him, while always the gentle voice breathed the tender words to her—*"My little darling!"*

So calmly, peacefully, quietly, he passed from us at the dawn on Wednesday, January 24, 1912. "Passed from us," did I say? Nay, only the outer garment has passed from our mortal vision. He lives! and when the great grief that tears our hearts at the separation is calmed and stilled, I think that we shall know that he is still with us. We shall again rejoice in his companionship and presence.

When his voice was growing faint and low, I heard him whispering, and leaning down to catch the words I heard—"At last, at last—at home—my wanderings are over"—and then, I heard no more, for my heart was breaking within me, and I felt, for *him* indeed it was *"Home at last!"* but for me—And then, as though he knew my thoughts, he turned and again holding out his hands to me, he said: "I have only one thing more to say to you, my beloved, and that is I love you, and I will be waiting for you; good-bye."

I write this memoir for those who love him, for those who will read it with tender loving hearts, and tearful eyes; for those who will not look critically at the way in which I have tried to tell out of my lonely heart this short story of his life and passing away—for *his* pupils, and, therefore, my friends.

We clothed the mortal remains in *pure white linen*, symbol of his fair, pure life, and so, clasping the photo of the one he loved best upon his bosom—they committed all that remained to the funeral pyre.

About the Author

James Allen was one of the pioneering figures of the self-help movement and modern inspirational thought. A philosophical writer and poet, he is best known for his book *As a Man Thinketh*. Writing about complex subjects such as faith, destiny, love, patience, and religion, he had the unique ability to explain them in a way that is simple and easy to comprehend. He often wrote about cause and effect, as well as overcoming sadness, sorrow and grief.

Allen was born in 1864 in Leicester, England into a working-class family. His father travelled alone to America to find work, but was murdered within days of arriving. With the family now facing economic disaster, Allen, at age 15, was forced to leave school and find work to support them.

During stints as a private secretary and stationer, he found that he could showcase his spiritual and social interests in journalism by writing for the magazine *The Herald of the Golden Age.*

In 1901, when he was 37, Allen published his first book, *From Poverty to Power.* In 1902 he began to publish his own spiritual magazine, *The Light of Reason* (which would be retitled *The Epoch* after his death). Each issue contained announcements, an editorial written by Allen on a different subject each month, and many articles, poems, and quotes written by popular authors of the day and even local, unheard of authors.

His third and most famous book *As a Man Thinketh* was published in 1903. The book's minor popularity enabled him to quit his secretarial work and pursue his writing and editing career full time. He wrote 19 books in all, publishing at least one per year while continuing to publish his magazine, until his death. Allen wrote when he had a message—one that he had lived out in his own life and knew that it was good.

In 1905, Allen organized his magazine subscribers into groups (called "The Brotherhood") that would meet regularly and reported on their meetings each month in the magazine. Allen and his wife, Lily Louisa Oram, whom he had married in 1895, would often travel to these group meetings to give speeches and read articles. Some of Allen's favorite writings, and those he quoted often, include the works of Shakespeare, Milton, Emerson, the Bible, Buddha, Whitman, Trine, and Lao-Tze.

Allen died in 1912 at the age of 47. Following his death, Lily, with the help of their daughter, Nora took over the editing of *The Light of Reason*, now under the name *The Epoch*. Lily continued to publish the magazine until her failing eyesight prevented her from doing so. Lily's life was devoted to spreading the works of her husband until her death at age 84.